Super Easy Air Fryer Cookbook

A Complete Cookbook To Prepare Better, Tastier And Faster Air Fryer Dishes For Yourself And Your Family

Megan Miller

Disclaimer Notice:

Please note the information contained within this document is for educational and entertainment purposes only. All effort has been executed to present accurate, up to date, and reliable, complete information. No warranties of any kind are declared or implied. Readers acknowledge that the author is not engaging in the rendering of legal, financial, medical or professional advice. The content within this book has been derived from various sources. Please consult a licensed professional before attempting any techniques outlined in this book.

By reading this document, the reader agrees that under no circumstances is the author responsible for any losses, direct or indirect, which are incurred as a result of the use of information contained within this document, including, but not limited to, — errors, omissions, or inaccuracies

Table Of Content

Introduction

Congratulations on purchasing your copy of ***Super Easy Air Fryer Cookbook: A Complete Cookbook To Prepare Better, Tastier And Faster Air Fryer Dishes For Yourself And Your Family*** , and thank you for doing so.

I'm glad that you have chosen to take this opportunity to welcome the **Air Fryer Diet** into your life. I'm sure this book will help you find all the information and tools you need to better integrate the **Air Fryer Diet** plan with your habits.

Also, I thought I would share with you some delicious ideas and recipes for all tastes and for the best of your low carb diet, which I hope you will appreciate.

You will find hundreds of easy to realize ideas that will best suit your situation or your needs at the moment, with all the preparation time, amount of servings, and the list of all the nutritional values you'll need.

BREAKFAST

Chopped Kale with Ground Beef

Preparation time: 12 minutes Cooking time: 16 minutes

Servings: 4

INGREDIENT

- 12 oz kale
- 1 cup ground beef
- ½ teaspoon salt
- ½ onion, diced
- 1 teaspoon ground paprika
- ¼ teaspoon minced garlic
- 1 teaspoon dried dill
- 1 teaspoon olive oil
- 1 oz almonds, crushed

DIRECTIONS

1. Mix up together the salt, diced onion, ground paprika, minced garlic, and dried dill in the mixing bowl.
2. Add the olive oil and stir carefully.
3. After this, place the ground beef in the air fryer basket.
4. Add the olive oil mixture. Stir it carefully.
5. Cook the ground beef for 13 minutes at 370 F. Stir it time to time.
6. Meanwhile, chop the kale.
7. Add the kale and crushed almonds in the

ground beef.

8. Stir it and cook for 3 minutes more at 350 F.

9. Then transfer the cooked meal in the serving bowls and serve!

NUTRITION: Calories 180, Fat 7.5, Fiber 2.7, Carbs 12.2, Protein 17.2

Turkey Tortillas

Preparation time: 5 minutes • Cooking time: 14 minutes • Servings: 4

INGREDIENTS

- 1 pound turkey breast, skinless, boneless, ground and browned
- 4 corn tortillas
- Cooking spray
- 1 cup cherry tomatoes, halved
- 1 cup kalamata olives, pitted and halved
- 1 cup corn
- 1 cup baby spinach
- 1 cup cheddar cheese, shredded
- Salt and black pepper to the taste

DIRECTIONS

1. Divide the meat, tomatoes and the other ingredients except the cooking spray on each tortilla, roll and grease them with the cooking spray
2. Preheat the air fryer at 350 degrees F, put the tortillas in the air fryer's basket, cook for 7 minutes on each side, divide between plates and serve for breakfast.

NUTRITION: Calories 244, Fat 11, Fiber 4, Carbs 5, Protein 7

Turkey and Peppers Bowls

Preparation time: 5 minutes • Cooking time: 20 minutes • Servings: 4

INGREDIENTS

- 1 red bell pepper, cut into strips
- 1-pound turkey breast, skinless, boneless, ground
- 4 eggs, whisked
- Salt and black pepper to the taste
- 1 cup corn
- 1 cup black olives, pitted and halved
- 1 cup mild salsa
- Cooking spray

DIRECTIONS

1. Heat up the air fryer at 350 degrees F, grease it with cooking spray, add the meat, peppers and the other ingredients, toss and cook for 20 minutes.
2. Divide into bowls and serve for breakfast.

NUTRITION: Calories 229, Fat 13, Fiber 3, Carbs 4, Protein 7

Bacon Wrapped Chicken Fillet

Preparation time: 15 minutes • Cooking time: 15 minutes • Servings: 6

INGREDIENTS

- 15 oz chicken fillet
- 6 oz bacon, sliced
- ½ teaspoon salt
- 1 teaspoon paprika
- 1 tablespoon olive oil
- 1 garlic clove, chopped

DIRECTIONS

1. Rub the chicken fillet with the salt, paprika, garlic clove and olive oil.
2. Wrap the rubbed chicken fillet in the bacon and secure gently with the toothpicks.
3. Place the chicken fillets in the air fryer basket.
4. Cook the chicken for 15 minutes at 380 F. Stir the chicken every 5 minutes.
5. Then slice the cooked chicken fillet and serve!

NUTRITION: Calories 310, Fat 19.5, Fiber 0.1, Carbs 0.8, Protein 31.1

Meatball Breakfast Salad

Preparation time: 15 minutes Cooking time: 10 minutes
Servings: 2

INGREDIENTS

- 1 cucumber, chopped
- 1 tomato, chopped
- 1 sweet red pepper, chopped
- ½ cup ground chicken
- 1 egg
- 1 tablespoon olive oil
- 2/3 teaspoon minced garlic
- ½ teaspoon ground black pepper

DIRECTIONS

1. Put the cucumber, tomato, and sweet red pepper in the mixing bowl.
2. Add olive oil and stir gently.
3. After this, mix up together the ground black pepper, minced garlic, and ground chicken.
4. Beat the egg in the chicken mixture and stir well. Make the medium meatballs.
5. After this, place the ground chicken meatballs in the air fryer basket and cook it for 10 minutes at 375 F.
6. Stir the ground chicken meatballs time to time.

7. Then chill the meatballs and add them in the salad.

8. Serve the breakfast immediately!

NUTRITION: Calories 208, Fat 12.2, Fiber 2.1, Carbs 12, Protein 14.

Cherry Tomatoes Fritatta

Preparation time: 10 minutes • Cooking time: 15 minutes •
Servings: 2

INGREDIENTS

- ¼ cup cherry tomatoes
- 1 tablespoon basil, chopped
- 3 eggs
- 2 tablespoon almond milk
- 1 teaspoon olive oil
- ¼ teaspoon turmeric
- 1 tablespoon almond flour

DIRECTIONS

1. Beat the eggs and whisk them well.
2. Add the chopped basil and almond milk.
1. Then add the almond flour and turmeric.
2. Stir the mixture well.
3. After this, cut the cherry tomatoes into the halves.
4. Pour the whisked egg mixture in the air fryer basket.
5. Add the cherry tomatoes.
6. Cook the frittata for 15 minutes at 355 F.
7. Then let the cooked frittata chill little.
8. Serve!

NUTRITION: Calories 234, Fat 19.6, Fiber 2.2, Carbs 5.4, Protein 11.9

MAIN

Cheese Burger Patties

Cooking Time: 15 minutes • Servings: 6

INGREDIENTS

- 1lb. ground beef
- 6cheddar cheese slices
- Pepper and salt to taste

DIRECTIONS

1. Preheat your air fryer to 390°Fahrenheit. Season beef with salt and pepper. Make six round shaped patties from the mixture and place them into air fryer basket. Air fry the patties for 10-minutes. Open the air fryer basket and place cheese slices on top of patties and place into air fryer with an additional cook time of 1-minute.

NUTRITION: Calories: 253, Total Fat: 14g, Carbs: 0.4g, Protein: 29g

Grilled Cheese Corn

Cooking Time: 15 minutes • Servings: 2

INGREDIENTS

- 2whole corn on the cob, peel husks and discard silk
- 1teaspoon olive oil
- 2teaspoons paprika
- ½ cup feta cheese, grated

DIRECTIONS

1. Rub the olive oil over corn then sprinkle with paprika and rub all over the corn. Preheat your air fryer to 300°Fahrenheit. Place the seasoned corn on the grill for 15-minutes. Place corn on a serving dish then sprinkle with grated cheese over corn. Serve and enjoy!

NUTRITION: Calories: 150, Total Fat: 10g, Carbs: 7g, Protein: 7g

Eggplant Fries

Cooking Time: 20 minutes • Servings: 4

INGREDIENTS

- 1eggplant, cut into 3-inch pieces
- ¼ cup of water
- 1tablespoon of olive oil
- 4tablespoons cornstarch
- sea salt to taste

DIRECTIONS

1. Preheat your air fryer to 390°Fahrenheit. In a bowl, combine eggplant, water, oil and cornstarch. Place the eggplant fries in air fryer basket, and air fry them for 20- minutes. Serve warm and enjoy!

Pineapple Pizza

Cooking Time: 10 minutes • Servings: 3

INGREDIENTS

- 1large whole wheat tortilla
- ¼ cup tomato pizza sauce
- ¼ cup pineapple tidbits
- ¼ cup mozzarella cheese, grated
- ¼ cup ham slice

DIRECTIONS

1. Preheat your air fryer to 300°Fahrenehit. Place the tortilla on a baking sheet then spread pizza sauce over tortilla. Arrange ham slice, cheese, pineapple over the tortilla. Place the pizza in the air fryer basket and cook for 10-minutes. Serve hot

   o

NUTRITION: Calories: 80, Total Fat: 2g, Carbs: 12g, Protein: 4g

Air Fryer Tortilla Pizza

Cooking Time: 7 minutes • Servings: 6

INGREDIENTS

- 1large whole wheat tortilla
- 1tablespoon black olives
- Salt and pepper to taste
- 4tablespoons tomato sauce
- 8pepperoni slices
- 3tablespoons of sweet corn
- 1medium, tomato, chopped
- ½ cup mozzarella cheese, grated

DIRECTIONS

1. Preheat your air fryer to 325°Fahrenheit. Spread tomato sauce over tortilla. Add pepperoni slices, olives, corn, tomato, and cheese on top of the tortilla. Season with salt and pepper. Place pizza in air fryer basket and cook for 7-minutes. Serve and enjoy!

NUTRITION: Calories: 110, Total Fat: 5g, Carbs: 10g, Protein: 4g

Air Fried Pork Apple Balls

Cooking Time: 15 minutes • Servings: 8

INGREDIENTS

- 2cups pork, minced
- 6basil leaves, chopped
- 2tablespoons cheddar cheese, grated
- 4garlic cloves, minced
- ½ cup apple, peeled, cored, chopped
- 1large white onion, diced
- Salt and pepper to taste
- 2teaspoons Dijon Mustard
- 1teaspoon liquid Stevia

DIRECTIONS

1. Add pork minced in a bowl then add diced onion and apple into a bowl and mix well. Add the stevia, mustard, garlic, cheese, basil, salt and pepper and combine well. Make small round balls from the mixture and place them into air fryer basket. Cook at 350°Fahrenheit for 15-minutes. Serve and enjoy!

Rotisserie Style Chicken

Cooking Time: 60 minutes • Servings: 4

INGREDIENTS

- 1whole chicken (under 6 lbs.
- Olive oil
- Seasoned salt

DIRECTIONS

1. Coat the chicken with olive oil. Season the chicken with salt. Cook in air fryer at 350°Fahrenheit for 30-minutes, then flip the chicken over and cook for an additional 30-minutes.

NUTRITION: Calories: 326, Total Fat: 22g, Carbs: 5g, Protein: 48g

Zucchini Manicotti

Cooking Time: 15 minutes Servings: 4

INGREDIENTS

- 2tablespoons fresh basil, chopped
- 1½ cups mozzarella, shredded
- 1cup marinara sauce
- 4medium zucchinis, sliced ¼-inch thick
- Salt and pepper to taste
- ½ teaspoon Italian seasoning
- 1clove garlic, minced
- 1large egg, lightly beaten
- 1cup parmesan cheese, grated
- 1½ cups ricotta

DIRECTIONS

1. In a mixing bowl, combine ½ cup parmesan, ricotta, egg, garlic and Italian seasoning. Season with salt and pepper and mix well. On a clean working surface place three slices of zucchini so they are slightly overlapping. Add a spoonful of ricotta mixture on top. Roll up and transfer to a greased air fryer baking dish. Repeat with remaining zucchini and ricotta mixture. Add the marinara sauce on top of the zucchini manicotti, then sprinkle all over with the remaining ½ cup

parmesan and mozzarella. Bake in the air fryer at 350°Fahrenheit for 15- minutes. Use fresh basil as garnish and serve right away.

NUTRITION: Calories: 356, Total Fat: 12.4g, Carbs: 10.2g, Protein: 34.2g

Steamed Salmon with Dill Sauce

Cooking Time: 15 minutes • Servings: 2

INGREDIENTS

- Sea salt about 2 pinches
- 2teaspoons olive oil
- 2tablespoons of dill, chopped
- ½ cup plain Greek yogurt
- ½ cup light sour cream
- 12-ounce salmon fillet

DIRECTIONS

1. First, set your air fryer to 300°Fahrenheit. Add one cup of water to the bottom of air
2. fryer. Cut the salmon into pieces and sprinkle one tablespoon of olive oil in the bowl and
3. mix with a pinch of salt. Add the pieces of salmon to the air fryer and cook for 12
4. minutes. Combine the chopped dill, salt, yogurt, sour cream in a bowl. Save
5. a teaspoon of chopped dill to garnish the top of the salmon.

NUTRITION: Calories: 278, Total Fat: 12.2g, Carbs: 8.2g, Protein: 34.2g

SIDES

Curry Cabbage

Preparation Time: 25 minutes

Servings: 4

Ingredients:

- 30 oz. green cabbage; shredded

- 3 tbsp. coconut oil; melted

- 1 tbsp. red curry paste

- A pinch of salt and black pepper

Directions:

1. In a pan that fits the air fryer, combine the cabbage with the rest of the ingredients, toss, introduce the pan in the machine and cook at 380°F for 20 minutes

2. Divide between plates and serve as a side dish.

Nutrition: Calories: 180; Fat: 14g; Fiber: 4g; Carbs: 6g; Protein: 8g

Kale and Pine Nuts

Preparation Time: 20 minutes

Servings: 4

Ingredients:

- 10 cups kale; torn

- 1/3 cup pine nuts

- 2 tbsp. lemon zest; grated

- 1 tbsp. lemon juice

- 2 tbsp. olive oil

- Salt and black pepper to taste.

Directions:

1. In a pan that fits the air fryer, combine all the ingredients, toss, introduce the pan in the machine and cook at 380°F for 15 minutes

2. Divide between plates and serve as a side dish.

Nutrition: Calories: 121; Fat: 9g; Fiber: 2g; Carbs: 4g; Protein: 5g

Artichoke Hearts and Tarragon

Preparation Time: 20 minutes

Servings: 4

Ingredients:

- 12 oz. artichoke hearts

- 2 tbsp. tarragon; chopped.

- 4 tbsp. butter; melted

- Juice of ½ lemon

- Salt and black pepper to taste.

Directions:

1. Take a bowl and mix all the ingredients, toss, transfer the artichokes to your air fryer's basket and cook at 370°F for 15 minutes

2. Divide between plates and serve as a side dish.

Nutrition: Calories: 200; Fat: 7g; Fiber: 2g; Carbs: 3g; Protein: 7g

SEAFOOD

Sage Shrimp

Preparation time: 3 minutes • Cooking time: 10 minutes •
Servings: 4

INGREDIENTS

- 2pounds shrimp, peeled and deveined
- 1tablespoon sage, chopped
- ½ cup chicken stock
- 4garlic cloves, minced
- Salt and black pepper to the taste
- 1tablespoon dill, chopped

DIRECTIONS

1. In the air fryer, mix the shrimp with the sage and
   the other ingredients, toss, cook at 360 degrees
   F for 10 minutes, divide into bowls and serve.

NUTRITION: Calories 210, Fat 11, Fiber 12, Carbs 16,
Protein 9

Salmon and Parsnips

Preparation time: 10 minutes • Cooking time: 20 minutes • Servings: 4

INGREDIENTS

- 4salmon fillets, boneless
- 1cup parsnips, peeled and cubed
- Juice of 1 lime
- 1tablespoon olive oil
- ¼ cup veggie stock
- 1teaspoon sweet paprika
- Salt and black pepper to the taste

DIRECTIONS

1. In your air fryer, mix the salmon with the parsnips and the other ingredients, cook at 370 degrees F for 20 minutes, divide everything between plates and serve.

NUTRITION: Calories 200, Fat 6, Fiber 6, Carbs 18, Protein 11

Spiced Cod

Preparation time: 4 minutes • Cooking time: 20 minutes •
Servings: 4

INGREDIENTS

- 4cod fillets, boneless
- 1teaspoon nutmeg, ground
- 1teaspoon allspice, ground
- 1teaspoon cinnamon powder
- 1teaspoon turmeric powder
- Juice of 1 lemon
- 1tablespoon avocado oil
- Salt and black pepper to the taste

DIRECTIONS

1. In your air fryer, mix the cod with the spices and
   the other ingredients, cook at
   370 degrees F for 20 minutes, divide between
   plates and serve.

NUTRITION: Calories 200, Fat 4, Fiber 8, Carbs 16,
Protein 7

Dill Sea Bass

Preparation time: 10 minutes • Cooking time: 14 minutes •
Servings: 4

INGREDIENTS

- 1pound sea bass fillets, boneless
- 1tablespoon olive oil
- 1tablespoon dill, chopped
- Salt and black pepper to the taste
- ½ teaspoon cumin, ground
- ½ teaspoon rosemary, dried
- 1tablespoon lemon juice

DIRECTIONS

1. In your air fryer, mix the sea bass with the oil, dill and the other ingredients, toss and cook at 360 degrees F for 14 minutes.
2. Divide the fish between plates and serve.

NUTRITION: Calories 280, Fat 11, Fiber 1, Carbs 12, Protein 18

Chervil Cod

Preparation time: 10 minutes • Cooking time: 20 minutes •
Servings: 4

INGREDIENTS

- 4cod fillets, boneless
- 1tablespoon chervil, chopped
- Juice of 1 lime
- Salt and black pepper to the taste
- ½ cup coconut milk
- A drizzle of olive oil

DIRECTIONS

1. In a baking dish that fits your air fryer, mix the cod with the chervil and the other ingredients, toss gently, introduce in your air fryer and cook at 380 degrees F for 20 minutes.
2. Divide between plates and serve hot.

NUTRITION: Calories 250, Fat 5, Fiber 6, Carbs 15, Protein 18

Honey Salmon

Preparation time: 5 minutes • Cooking time: 15 minutes • Servings: 4

INGREDIENTS

- 4salmon fillets, boneless
- 2tablespoons lemon juice
- A pinch of salt and black pepper
- 1tablespoon honey
- 2tablespoons olive oil
- 2tablespoons chives, chopped

DIRECTIONS

1. In the air fryer's pan, mix the salmon with the lemon juice, honey and the other ingredients and cook at 350 degrees F for 15 minutes.
2. Divide the mix between plates and serve.

NUTRITION: Calories 272, Fat 8, Fiber 12, Carbs 15, Protein 16

POULTRY

Chicken and Coriander Sauce

Preparation time: 10 minutes • Cooking time: 25 minutes • Servings: 4

INGREDIENTS

- 2pounds chicken breast, skinless, boneless and sliced
- 1cup cilantro, chopped
- Juice of 1 lime
- ½ cup heavy cream
- 1tablespoon olive oil
- ½ teaspoon cumin, ground
- 1teaspoon sweet paprika
- 5garlic cloves, chopped
- 1cup chicken stock
- A pinch of salt and black pepper

DIRECTIONS

1. In a blender, mix the cilantro with the lime juice and the other ingredients except the chicken and the stock and pulse well.
2. Put the chicken, stock and sauce in the air fryer's pan, toss, introduce the pan in the fryer and cook at 380 degrees F for 25 minutes.
3. Divide the mix between plates and serve

NUTRITION: Calories 261, Fat 12, Fiber 7, Carbs 15, Protein 25

Turkey Chili

Preparation time: 10 minutes • Cooking time: 25 minutes • Servings: 4

INGREDIENTS

- 1pound turkey breast, skinless, boneless and cubed
- 1red onion, chopped
- 1red chili pepper, minced
- 1cup tomato sauce
- 1teaspoon chili powder
- Salt and black pepper to the taste
- 1teaspoon cumin, ground
- 1cup chicken stock

DIRECTIONS

1. In a pan that fits your air fryer, mix the turkey with the onion and the other ingredients, stir, introduce in the fryer and cook at 380 degrees F for 25 minutes.
2. Divide into bowls and serve.

NUTRITION: Calories 251, Fat 8, Fiber 8, Carbs 15, Protein 17

Chicken Stew

Preparation time: 10 minutes • Cooking time: 40 minutes • Servings: 4

INGREDIENTS

- 2pounds chicken breast, skinless, boneless and cubed
- 1cup canned tomatoes, crushed
- 1tablespoon olive oil
- 2carrots, peeled and sliced
- 1parsnip, peeled and sliced
- 1tablespoon ginger, grated
- 1chili pepper, minced
- 1cup chicken stock
- Salt and black pepper to the taste

DIRECTIONS

1. In the air fryer's pan, mix the chicken with the tomatoes and the other ingredients, toss, cook at 400 degrees F for 40 minutes, divide into bowls and serve

NUTRITION: Calories 270, Fat 8, Fiber 4, Carbs 20, Protein 17

Pepper Chicken Mix

Preparation time: 10 minutes • Cooking time: 25 minutes • Servings: 4

INGREDIENTS:

- 2pounds chicken breasts, skinless and boneless
- 1teaspoon red pepper flakes, crushed
- 1teaspoon cayenne pepper
- 2tablespoons lemon juice
- Salt and black pepper to the taste
- ½ teaspoon lemon pepper
- 1tablespoon olive oil

DIRECTIONS

1. In the air fryer's pan, mix the chicken with the red pepper flakes and the other ingredients, transfer this to your air fryer, cook at 360 degrees F for 25 minutes, divide between plates and serve with a side salad.

NUTRITION: Calories 240, Fat 7, Fiber 1, Carbs 17, Protein 18

Chicken and Pears Mix

Preparation time: 10 minutes • Cooking time: 25 minutes • Servings: 4

INGREDIENTS

- 1pound chicken breasts, skinless, boneless and halved
- 2pears, cored and cubed
- 1cup white wine
- 2tablespoons balsamic vinegar
- 2garlic cloves, minced
- 1tablespoon chives, chopped
- Salt and black pepper to the taste
- 1teaspoon sweet paprika

DIRECTIONS

1. In the air fryer's pan, mix the chicken with the pears and the other ingredients, and cook at 370 degrees F for 25 minutes.
2. Divide everything between plates and serve.

NUTRITION: Calories 271, Fat 12, Fiber 3, Carbs 17, Protein 15

Chicken and Chili Sauce

Preparation time: 10 minutes • Cooking time: 25 minutes • Servings: 4

INGREDIENTS

- 2pounds chicken breast, skinless, boneless and cubed
- 1tablespoon chili paste
- 1red chili, minced
- ½ teaspoon smoked paprika
- 1teaspoon mustard powder
- Salt and black pepper to the taste
- ½ cup chicken stock

DIRECTIONS

1. In the air fryer's pan, mix the chicken with the chili paste and the other ingredients, cook at 370 degrees F for 25 minutes, divide everything between plates and serve.

NUTRITION: Calories 283, Fat 13, Fiber 7, Carbs 19, Protein 17

Chicken and Chickpeas

Preparation time: 10 minutes • Cooking time: 25 minutes • Servings: 4

INGREDIENTS:

- 1pound chicken breast, skinless, boneless and cubed
- 1cup canned chickpeas, drained
- 1cup tomato sauce
- Salt and black pepper to the taste
- 2teaspoons olive oil
- ½ teaspoon garlic powder
- ½ teaspoon coriander, ground
- 1teaspoon basil, dried
- 1tablespoon parsley, chopped

DIRECTIONS

1. In the air fryer's pan, mix the chicken with the chickpeas and the other ingredients, toss, introduce the pan in the fryer and cook at 370 degrees F for 25 minutes.
2. Divide the mix into bowls and serve.

NUTRITION: Calories 261, Fat 8, Fiber 6, Carbs 16, Protein 16

MEAT

Pork with Tomatoes and Cauliflower

Preparation time: 10 minutes

Cooking time: 25 minutes

Servings: 4

Ingredients:

- 2 pounds pork loin, boneless and cubed

- 1 cup cherry tomatoes, halved

- 1 cup cauliflower florets

- ¾ cup beef stock

- 2 tablespoons olive oil

- ½ tablespoon smoked paprika

- ½ tablespoon garlic powder

- Salt and black pepper to the taste

Directions:

1. Heat up the air fryer with the oil at 360 degrees F, add the pork loin, cherry tomatoes and the other ingredients, toss and cook for 25 minutes.

2. Divide everything between plates and serve.

Nutrition: calories 290, fat 11, fiber 6, carbs 20, protein 29

Sage Pork and Okra

Preparation time: 10 minutes

Cooking time: 25 minutes

Servings: 4

Ingredients:

- 2 pounds pork stew meat, cubed

- 2 tablespoons olive oil

- 1 cup okra, sliced

- 1 tablespoon sage, chopped

- 1 red onion, chopped

- 1 tablespoon sweet paprika

- Salt and black pepper to the taste

Directions:

1. Heat up the air fryer with the oil at 390 degrees F, add the onion, the meat and the other ingredients, toss and cook for 25 minutes.

2. Divide everything between plates and serve.

Nutrition: calories 291, fat 12, fiber 9, carbs 20, protein 26

Favorite Beef Stroganoff

Preparation Time: 20 minutes + marinating time

Servings: 4

Nutrition: 418 Calories; 25.8g Fat; 9g Carbs; 32.6g Protein; 1.4g Sugars; 1g Fiber

Ingredients

- 1 ¼ pounds beef sirloin steak, cut into small-sized strips

- 1/4 cup balsamic vinegar

- 1 tablespoon brown mustard

- 1 tablespoon butter

- 1 cup beef broth

- 1 cup leek, chopped

- 2 cloves garlic, crushed

- 1 teaspoon cayenne pepper

- Sea salt flakes and crushed red pepper, to taste

- 1 cup sour cream

- 2 ½ tablespoons tomato paste

Directions

1. Place the beef along with the balsamic vinegar and the mustard in a mixing dish; cover and marinate in your refrigerator for about 1 hour.

2. Butter the inside of a baking dish and put the beef into the dish.

3. Add the broth, leeks and garlic. Cook at 380 degrees for 8 minutes. Pause the machine and add the cayenne pepper, salt, red pepper, sour cream and tomato paste; cook for additional 7 minutes.

4. Bon appétit!

Shoulder Steak with Herbs and Brussels Sprouts

Preparation Time: 30 minutes + marinating time

Servings: 4

Nutrition: 302 Calories; 14.2g Fat; 6.5g Carbs; 36.6g Protein; 1.6g Sugars; 2.8g Fiber

Ingredients

- 1 pound beef chuck shoulder steak

- 2 tablespoons vegetable oil

- 1 tablespoon red wine vinegar

- 1 teaspoon fine sea salt

- 1/2 teaspoon ground black pepper

- 1 teaspoon smoked paprika

- 1 teaspoon onion powder

- 1/2 teaspoon garlic powder

- 1/2 pound Brussels sprouts, cleaned and halved

- 1/2 teaspoon fennel seeds

- 1 teaspoon dried basil

- 1 teaspoon dried sage

Directions

1. Firstly, marinate the beef with vegetable oil, wine vinegar, salt, black pepper, paprika, onion powder, and garlic powder. Rub the marinade into the meat and let it stay at least for 3 hours.

2. Air fry at 390 degrees F for 10 minutes. Pause the machine and add the prepared Brussels sprouts; sprinkle them with fennel seeds, basil, and sage.

3. Turn the machine to 380 degrees F; press the power button and cook for 5 more minutes. Pause the machine, stir and cook for further 10 minutes.

4. Next, remove the meat from the cooking basket and cook the vegetables a few minutes more if needed and according to your taste. Serve with your favorite mayo sauce.

Keto Wiener Schnitzel

Preparation Time: 20 minutes

Servings: 2

Nutrition: 540 Calories; 33.6g Fat; 1.8g Carbs; 59g Protein; 0.7g Sugars; 0.6g Fiber

Ingredients

- 1 egg, beaten

- 1/2 teaspoon ground black pepper

- 1 teaspoon paprika

- 1/2 teaspoon coarse sea salt

- 1 tablespoon ghee, melted

- 1/2 cup Romano cheese, grated

- 2 beef schnitzel

Directions

1. Start by preheating your Air Fryer to 360 degrees F.

2. In a shallow bowl, whisk the egg with black pepper, paprika, and salt.

3. Thoroughly combine the ghee with the Romano cheese in another shallow bowl. Using a meat mallet, pound the schnitzel to 1/4-inch thick.

4. Dip the schnitzel into the egg mixture; then, roll the schnitzel over the Romano cheese mixture until coated on all sides.

5. Cook for 13 minutes in the preheated Air Fryer. Bon appétit!

Short Ribs in Spicy Red Sauce

Preparation Time: 20 minutes + marinating time

Servings: 4

Nutrition: 397 Calories; 15.7g Fat; 4.9g Carbs; 35.2g Protein; 2g Sugars; 1.2g Fiber

Ingredients

- 1 ½ pounds short ribs

- 1 cup red wine

- 1 lemon, juiced

- 1 teaspoon fresh ginger, grated

- 1 teaspoon salt

- 1 teaspoon black pepper

- 1 teaspoon paprika

- 1 teaspoon chipotle chili powder

- 1 cup tomato paste

- 1 teaspoon garlic powder

- 1 teaspoon cumin

Directions

1. In a ceramic bowl, place the beef ribs, wine, lemon juice, ginger, salt, black pepper, paprika, and chipotle chili powder. Cover and let it marinate for 3 hours in the refrigerator.

2. Discard the marinade and add the short ribs to the Air Fryer basket. Cook in the preheated Air fry at 380 degrees F for 10 minutes, turning them over halfway through the cooking time.

3. In the meantime, heat the saucepan over medium heat; add the reserved marinade and stir in the tomato paste, garlic powder, and cumin. Cook until the sauce has thickened slightly.

4. Pour the sauce over the warm ribs and serve immediately. Bon appétit!

EGGS AND DAIRY

Greek Frittata with Feta Cheese

Preparation Time: 10 minutes

Servings: 4

Nutrition: 221 Calories; 10.7g Fat; 2.1g Carbs; 27g Protein; 1.1g Sugars; 0.3g Fiber

Ingredients

- 1/3 cup Feta cheese, crumbled

- 1 teaspoon dried rosemary

- 2 tablespoons fish sauce

- 1 ½ cup cooked chicken breasts, boneless and shredded

- 1/2 teaspoon coriander sprig, finely chopped

- 6 medium-sized whisked eggs

- 1/3 teaspoon ground white pepper

- 1 cup fresh chives, chopped

- 1/2 teaspoon garlic paste

- Fine sea salt, to taste

- Nonstick cooking spray

Directions

1. Grab a baking dish that fit in your Air Fryer.

—

2. Lightly coat the inside of the baking dish with a nonstick cooking spray of choice. Stir in all ingredients, minus feta cheese. Stir to combine well.

3. Set your Air Fryer to cook at 335 degrees for 8 minutes; check for doneness. Scatter crumbled feta over the top and eat immediately!

VEGETABLE

Broccoli with Olives

Preparation Time: 15 minutes

Cooking time: 19 minutes

Servings: 4

Ingredients:

- 2 pounds broccoli, stemmed and cut into 1-inch florets

- 1/3 cup Kalamata olives, halved and pitted

- ¼ cup Parmesan cheese, grated

- 2 tablespoons olive oil

- Salt and ground black pepper, as required

- 2 teaspoons fresh lemon zest, grated

Directions:

1. Preheat the Air fryer to 400 0 F and grease an Air fryer basket.

2. Boil the broccoli for about 4 minutes and drain well.

3. Mix broccoli, oil, salt, and black pepper in a bowl and toss to coat well.

4. Arrange broccoli into the Air fryer basket and cook for about 15 minutes.

5. Stir in the olives, lemon zest and cheese and dish out to serve.

Nutrition:

Calories: 169, Fat: 10.2g, Carbohydrates: 16g, Sugar: 3.9g, Protein: 8.5g, Sodium: 254mg

Spiced Eggplant

Preparation Time: 15 minutes

Cooking time: 27 minutes

Servings: 3

Ingredients:

- 2 medium eggplants, cubed

- 2 tablespoons butter, melted

- 2 tablespoons Parmesan cheese, shredded

- 1 tablespoon Maggi seasoning sauce

- 1 teaspoon sumac

- 1 teaspoon garlic powder

- 1 teaspoon onion powder

- Salt and ground black pepper, as required

- 1 tablespoon fresh lemon juice

Directions:

1. Preheat the Air fryer to 320 0 F and grease an Air fryer basket.

2. Mix the eggplant cubes, butter, seasoning sauce and spices in a bowl and toss to coat well.

3. Arrange the eggplant cubes in the Air fryer basket and cook for about 15 minutes.

4. Dish out in a bowl and set the Air fryer to 350 o F.

5. Cook for about 12 minutes, tossing once in between.

6. Dish out in a bowl and sprinkle with lemon juice and Parmesan cheese to serve.

Nutrition:

Calories: 173, Fat: 8.9g, Carbohydrates: 23g, Sugar: 11.6g, Protein: 4.6g, Sodium: 276mg

SNACK

Beef Meatballs in Blueberry Chipotle Sauce

Cooking Time: 20 minutes • Servings: 4

INGREDIENTS

- 2tablespoons Dijon mustard
- Salt and black pepper to taste
- 1tablespoon herb vinegar
- ½ teaspoon cumin
- 1teaspoon liquid stevia
- 1½ teaspoons garlic, minced
- ½ lb. ground beef
- 1/3 cup blueberry chipotle ketchup
- 2tablespoons scallions, minced
- 1½ Worcestershire sauce

DIRECTIONS

1. In a large dish mix meat, cumin, scallions, salt, pepper, combine well. Form meatballs and cook them in your air-fryer at   375°Fahrenheit for 15- minutes. Meanwhile, add the other ingredients into a pan over medium heat and cook for 5- minutes. Add the meatballs to pan and stir, cook for an additional 5-inutes.

NUTRITION: Calories: 112, Total Fat: 8.28g, Carbs: 2.4g, Protein: 9.75g

Lemon Pepper Broccoli Crunch

Preparation time: 5 minutes • Cooking time: 6 Hours •
Servings: 4

INGREDIENTS

- 4cups broccoli florets, chopped into bite sized pieces
- 1Tbsp olive oil
- 1tsp sea salt
- 1tsp lemon pepper seasoning

DIRECTIONS:

1. Preheat your air fryer to 135 degrees F.
2. Wash and drain the broccoli florets.
3. Place the broccoli in a large bowl and toss with the olive oil and sea salt.
4. Add the broccoli to the basket of your air fryer or spread them in a flat layer on the tray of your air fryer (either option will work!).
5. Cook in the air fryer for about 6 hours, tossing the broccoli every hour or so to cook evenly. Essentially, you will be dehydrating the broccoli.
6. Once the broccoli is fully dried, remove it from the air fryer, toss with the lemon pepper seasoning, and then let cool. It will keep crisping as it cools.
7. Enjoy fresh or store in an airtight container for up to a month.

NUTRITION: Calories 53, Total Fat 3g, Saturated Fat 0g, Total Carbs 3g, Net Carbs 1g, Protein 2g, Sugar 0g, Fiber 2g, Sodium 629mg, Potassium 0g

Sweet Broccoli Crunch

Preparation time: 5 minutes • Cooking time: 6 Hours • Servings: 4

INGREDIENTS

- 4cups broccoli florets, chopped into bite sized pieces
- 1Tbsp olive oil
- 1tsp sea salt
- 1tsp granulated erythritol

DIRECTIONS:

1. Preheat your air fryer to 135 degrees F.
2. Wash and drain the broccoli florets.
3. Place the broccoli in a large bowl and toss with the olive oil, erythritol, and sea salt.
4. Add the broccoli to the basket of your air fryer or spread them in a flat layer on the tray of your air fryer (either option will work!).
5. Cook in the air fryer for about 6 hours, tossing the broccoli every hour or so to cook evenly. Essentially, you will be dehydrating the broccoli.
6. Once the broccoli is fully dried, remove it from the air fryer and then let cool. It will keep crisping as it cools.
7. Enjoy fresh or store in an airtight container for up to a month.

NUTRITION: Calories 62, Total Fat 3g, Saturated Fat 0g, Total Carbs 5g, Net Carbs 2g, Protein 2g, Sugar 0g, Fiber 3g, Sodium 610mg, Potassium 0g

Maple Broccoli Crunch

Preparation time: 5 minutes • Cooking time: 6 Hours • Servings: 4

INGREDIENTS

- 4cups broccoli florets, chopped into bite sized pieces
- 1Tbsp olive oil
- 1tsp sea salt
- 1½ tsp maple extract

DIRECTIONS:

1. Preheat your air fryer to 135 degrees F.
2. Wash and drain the broccoli florets.
3. Place the broccoli in a large bowl and toss with the olive oil, maple extract, and sea salt.
4. Add the broccoli to the basket of your air fryer or spread them in a flat layer on the tray of your air fryer (either option will work!).
5. Cook in the air fryer for about 6 hours, tossing the broccoli every hour or so to cook evenly. Essentially, you will be dehydrating the broccoli.
6. Once the broccoli is fully dried, remove it from the air fryer and then let cool. It will keep crisping as it cools.

7. Enjoy fresh or store in an airtight container for up to a month.

NUTRITION: Calories 54, Total Fat 3g, Saturated Fat 0g, Total Carbs 3g, Net Carbs 1g, Protein 2g, Sugar 1g, Fiber 2g, Sodium 610mg, Potassium 0g

Toad in the Hole

Cooking Time: 30 minutes • Servings: 4

INGREDIENTS

- 1cup milk
- ½ cup cold water
- 1tablespoon basil, fresh sprigs
- 1red onion, finely sliced
- 1½ cups almond flour
- 8small sausages
- 1tablespoon olive oil
- 1clove of garlic, pressed

DIRECTIONS

1. Use an ovenproof dish that fits in your air-fryer and coat with oil. Sift the flour in a medium-sized bowl and beat the eggs into it. Gradually include the milk, water, the hacked onion and garlic and season to taste with salt and pepper. Combine everything. Pierce and stick the sprigs of basil into sausages and place into a dish. Pour the batter over sausages. Preheat your air-fryer to 300°Fahrenheit and cook for 30-minutes.

Glass Noodle & Tiger Shrimp Salad

Cooking Time: 8 minutes • Servings: 4

INGREDIENTS

- 12tiger shrimps, butterflied
- Zest of one lemon
- Zest of one lime
- ¼ cup olive oil
- 2tablespoons mixed spice
- 2tablespoons olive oil
- A handful of basil, fried for garnish
- For the salad:
- 4baby yellow bell peppers, sliced
- 4baby red bell peppers, sliced
- 2scallions, bias cut
- 2cups green papaya, peeled, seeded, julienned
- ½ cup mint leaves
- ½ cup cilantro leaves
- 16-ounces of glass noodles, cooked and chilled
- 1English cucumber, peeled, seeded, sliced
- 1carrot, peeled and julienned
- 2tablespoons basil leaves, julienned
- For dressing:
- 4-ounces of honey
- 2cups grapeseed oil

- 1cup soy sauce
- 4-ounces ginger, peeled and grated
- 1bunch scallions, sliced
- 2tablespoons of sweet chili sauce

DIRECTIONS

1. Preheat your air-fryer to 390°Fahrenheit for 10-minutes. Mix olive oil and mixed spice and brush mixture over shrimp. Sprinkle the lemon and lime juice over the shrimps. Season with salt and pepper. Place the shrimp in the basket and cook for 4-minutes. Chill shrimps on a plate and repeat cooking process with remaining shrimp. Whisk lemon juice, soy sauce, honey, ginger, scallion and sweet chili sauce in a bowl. Whisk in oil. Add mixture to blend and mix to get a puree consistency. Season to taste. In a bowl, toss mixed greens and salad dressing mix, along with noodles, then divide it between serving plates. Top each plate of salad with 3 shrimps. Garnish with cilantro and basil.

NUTRITION: Calories: 258, Total Fat: 15.89g, Carbs: 4.41g, Protein: 23.59g

Air-Fried Fingerling Potatoes

Cooking Time: 30 minutes • Servings: 4

INGREDIENTS

- 2lbs. Fingerling potatoes, peeled, cubed
- 2tablespoons chives, minced
- 2tablespoons parsley leaves, minced
- 2garlic cloves, smashed
- 2tablespoons butter, melted
- 1shallot, quartered

DIRECTIONS

1. Add cubed potatoes to an oven-proof dish. Brush potatoes with melted butter. Sprinkle with cubed potatoes the rest of ingredients. Set your air-fryer for 320°Fahrenheit and cook for 30-minutes. Stir a few times during cook time. Serve warm.

NUTRITION: Calories: 213, Total Fat: 5.2g, Carbs: 32.1g, Protein: 4.68g

Parmesan Chicken Meatballs

Cooking Time: 10 minutes • Servings: 4

INGREDIENTS

- ½ cup whole-wheat breadcrumbs
- Pepper and salt to taste
- ½ lime, zested
- 1/3 cup parmesan cheese, grated
- ½ teaspoon paprika
- 1teaspoon basil, dried
- 3garlic cloves, minced
- ½ lb. ground chicken
- 1/3 teaspoon mustard seeds
- 1½ tablespoons melted butter
- 2eggs, beaten

DIRECTIONS

1. In a non-stick skillet that is preheated over medium heat, place ground chicken, garlic and cook until chicken is no longer pink, about 5-minutes.

2. Throw the remaining ingredients into skillet. Remove from heat. Allow to cool down and roll into balls. Roll each ball into beaten eggs, then roll them in breadcrumbs and transfer them into the air-fryer basket. Cook for 8-minutes at

385°Fahrenheit.

NUTRITION: Calories: 52, Total Fat: 2.46g, Carbs: 2.94g, Protein: 7.8g

Fried Banana Turmeric Chips

Cooking Time: 8 minutes • Servings: 4

INGREDIENTS

- 1teaspoon of sesame oil
- ½ teaspoon pepper
- 1teaspoon turmeric
- 4large bananas, sliced
- ½ teaspoon salt
- 2teaspoons agave syrup

DIRECTIONS

1. In a bowl, mix agave syrup, and turmeric. Season with salt and pepper. Add sliced bananas and toss to combine. Set aside. Preheat your air- fryer to 370°Fahrenheit. Spray sesame oil over sliced bananas and place into the air-fryer basket. Cook bananas for 8- minutes, shake basket halfway through cook time. Serve warm.

NUTRITION: Calories: 176, Total Fat: 9.9g, Carbs: 23.4g, Protein: 1.13g

Spicy Air-Fried Eggplant

Cooking Time: 20 minutes • Servings: 4

INGREDIENTS

- 2garlic cloves, minced
- 2large eggplants, sliced
- 2red chili peppers, chopped
- 2green chili peppers, minced
- 1teaspoon sesame oil
- 1tablespoon light soy sauce
- Pepper and salt to taste

DIRECTIONS

1. Cut eggplants and set aside. Chop chilies and mince garlic and save for later use. In a bowl, mix garlic, green and red chili peppers. Add soy sauce and sprinkle with pepper, add eggplant slices, toss and set aside. Preheat your air-fryer to 350°Fahrenheit. Add eggplant slices and spray with sesame oil. Cook for 20- minutes, shake basket every 5-minutes during cook time. Once cooked garnish eggplant slices with chili peppers and garlic. Serve warm.

NUTRITION: Calories: 223, Total Fat: 6.4g, Carbs: 11.8g, Protein: 3.2g

Air-Fried Carrots with Lemon

Cooking Time: 18 minutes • Servings: 4

INGREDIENTS

- 2cups carrots (julienned
- 1tablespoon parsley, chopped
- 1teaspoon paprika
- 2teaspoon lemon juice
- ½ teaspoon pepper
- 1teaspoon salt
- 2teaspoons olive oil
- 1tablespoon lemon zest

DIRECTIONS

1. In a bowl, combine lemon zest, lemon juice, paprika, salt, pepper, olive oil, carrots, and toss. Combine ingredients and allow to stand for 30-minutes before air-frying.
2. Preheat air-fryer to 390°Fahrenheit. Add carrots to the air-fryer basket and cook for 18-minutes. Give the basket a shake a couple of times during the cook time. Serve warm.

NUTRITION: Calories: 201, Total Fat: 11.48g, Carbs: 25.3g, Protein: 1.08

Air-Fried Radish Cake

Cooking Time: 15 minutes • Servings: 4

INGREDIENTS

- 2cups radish, cut into big strips
- ¼ cup potato flour
- 1tablespoon Sriracha sauce
- 1teaspoon black pepper
- ½ teaspoon salt
- 1teaspoon olive oil
- 1tablespoon flax seed combined with 3 tablespoons water

DIRECTIONS

1. In a blender add the flax seed and water and blend until smooth. In a mixing bowl, add Sriracha sauce, salt, and pepper. Stir, add strips of radish. Add flax seed mix to the bowl and mix well. Add the potato flour to another bowl. Coat the radish sticks with flour and set aside.

2. Preheat your air-fryer to 350°Fahrenheit. Add coated radish to air-fryer and spray with olive oil. Cook for 15-minutes, shake a couple of times during cook time. Serve warm.

NUTRITION: Calories: 78, Total Fat: 6.07g, Carbs: 7.14g, Protein: 1.3g

DESSERT

Raisins Rice Mix

Preparation time: 10 minutes • Cooking time: 25 minutes • Servings: 6

INGREDIENTS

- 1cup white rice
- 2cups coconut milk
- 3tablespoons sugar
- 1teaspoon vanilla extract
- ½ cup raisins

DIRECTIONS:

1. In the air fryer's pan, combine the rice with the milk and the other ingredients, introduce the pan in the fryer and cook at 320 degrees F for 25 minutes.
2. Divide into bowls and serve warm.

NUTRITION: Calories 132, Fat 6, Fiber 7, Carbs 11, Protein 7

Zucchini Bread

Preparation time: 10 minutes • Cooking time: 40 minutes •
Servings: 8

INGREDIENTS

- 3tablespoons butter, melted
- 2tablespoons sugar
- 1teaspoon vanilla extract
- 1cup zucchinis, grated
- 2eggs, whisked
- 1teaspoon baking soda
- 2cups almond flour
- 1cup almond milk
- 1teaspoon almond extract

DIRECTIONS

1. In a bowl, mix the melted butter with the sugar and
   the other ingredients, stir, pour into a lined loaf
   pan, place the pan in the air fryer and cook at 340
   degrees F for 40 minutes
2. Cool down, slice and serve.

NUTRITION: Calories 222, Fat 7, Fiber 8, Carbs 14,
Protein 4

Orange Bowls

Preparation time: 10 minutes • Cooking time: 10 minutes •
Servings: 4

INGREDIENTS

- 1cup oranges, peeled and cut into segments
- 1cup cherries, pitted and halved
- 1cup mango, peeled and cubed
- 1cup orange juice
- 2tablespoon sugar

DIRECTIONS

1. In the air fryer's pan, mix the oranges with the cherries and the other ingredients, toss and cook at 320 degrees F for 10 minutes.
2. Divide into bowls and serve cold.

NUTRITION: Calories 191, Fat 7, Fiber 3, Carbs 14, Protein 4

Maple Pears Mix

Preparation time: 10 minutes • Cooking time: 15 minutes •
Servings: 4

INGREDIENTS

- 1pound pears, cored and cut into wedges
- 1teaspoon cinnamon powder
- ½ cup coconut cream
- ½ teaspoon nutmeg powder
- 1tablespoon maple syrup
- 2tablespoon sugar
- 1tablespoon coconut oil, melted

DIRECTIONS

1. In a pan that fits your air fryer, mix the pears with the cream and the other ingredients, toss, introduce the pan in the fryer and cook at 360 degrees F for 15 minutes.
2. Divide into bowls and serve.

NUTRITION: Calories 180, Fat 6, Fiber 8, Carbs 19, Protein 12

Cherry Squares

Preparation time: 10 minutes • Cooking time: 25 minutes • Servings: 12

INGREDIENTS:

- 4eggs, whisked
- 1cup cherries, pitted and chopped
- 1cup almond flour
- ½ cup cream cheese
- ½ cup coconut cream
- 1tablespoon sugar
- 2tablespoons cocoa powder
- 2teaspoons vanilla extract
- ½ teaspoon baking powder

DIRECTIONS

1. In a bowl, mix the eggs with the cherries and the other ingredients, whisk well, pour this into a lined baking dish that fits your air fryer, introduce in the fryer at 320 degrees F, bake for 25 minutes, cool down, cut into squares and serve.

NUTRITION: Calories 178, Fat 11, Fiber 3, Carbs 3, Protein 5

Cinnamon Bananas

Preparation time: 10 minutes • Cooking time: 15 minutes •
Servings: 4

INGREDIENTS

- 3tablespoons coconut butter
- 2tablespoons flax meal combined with 2 tablespoons water
- 8bananas, peeled and halved
- ½ cup corn flour
- 3tablespoons cinnamon powder
- 1cup vegan breadcrumbs

DIRECTIONS

1. Heat up a pan with the butter over medium-high heat, add breadcrumbs, stir and cook for 4 minutes and then transfer to a bowl.
2. Roll each banana in flour, flax meal and breadcrumbs mix.
3. Arrange bananas in your air fryer's basket, dust with cinnamon sugar and cook at 280 degrees F for 10 minutes.
4. Transfer to plates and serve.
5. Enjoy!

NUTRITION: Calories 214, Fat 1, Fiber 4, Carbs 12, Protein 4

Coffee Pudding

Preparation time: 10 minutes • Cooking time: 10 minutes •
Servings: 4

INGREDIENTS

- 4ounces coconut butter
- 4ounces dark vegan chocolate, chopped
- Juice of ½ orange
- 1teaspoon baking powder
- 2ounces whole wheat flour
- ½ teaspoon instant coffee
- 2tablespoons flax meal combined with 2 tablespoons water
- 2ounces coconut sugar

DIRECTIONS

1. Heat up a pan with the coconut butter over medium heat, add chocolate and orange juice, stir well and take off heat.
2. In a bowl, mix sugar with instant coffee and flax meal, beat using your mixer, add chocolate mix, flour, salt and baking powder and stir well.
3. Pour this into a greased pan, introduce in your air fryer, cook at 360 degrees F for 10 minutes, divide between plates and serve.

4. Enjoy!

NUTRITION: Calories 189, Fat 6, Fiber 4, Carbs 14, Protein 3

Almond and Cocoa Cake

Preparation time: 10 minutes • Cooking time: 30 minutes • Servings: 8

INGREDIENTS:

- 1and ½ cup stevia
- 1cup flour
- ¼ cup cocoa powder+ 2 tablespoons
- ½ cup chocolate almond milk
- 2teaspoons baking powder
- 2tablespoons canola oil
- 1teaspoon vanilla extract
- 1and ½ cups hot water
- Cooking spray

DIRECTIONS

1. In a bowl, mix flour with 2 tablespoons cocoa, baking powder, almond milk, oil and vanilla extract, whisk well and spread on the bottom of a cake pan greased with cooking spray.
2. In a separate bowl, mix stevia with the rest of the cocoa and the water, whisk well and spread over the batter in the pan.
3. Introduce in the fryer and cook at 350 degrees F for 30 minutes.
4. Leave the cake to cool down, slice and serve.

5. Enjoy!

NUTRITION: Calories 250, Fat 4, Fiber 3, Carbs 10, Protein 2

Blueberry Cake

Preparation time: 10 minutes • Cooking time: 30 minutes
•Servings: 6

INGREDIENTS

- ½ cup whole wheat flour
- ¼ teaspoon baking powder
- ¼ teaspoon stevia
- ¼ cup blueberries
- 1/3 cup almond milk
- 1teaspoon olive oil
- 1teaspoon flaxseed, ground
- ½ teaspoon lemon zest, grated
- ¼ teaspoon vanilla extract
- ¼ teaspoon lemon extract
- Cooking spray

DIRECTIONS

1. In a bowl, mix flour with baking powder, stevia, blueberries, milk, oil, flaxseeds, lemon zest, vanilla extract and lemon extract and whisk well.

2. Spray a cake pan with cooking spray, line it with parchment paper, pour cake batter, introduce in the fryer and cook at 350 degrees F for 30 minutes.

3. Leave the cake to cool down, slice and serve.

4. Enjoy!

NUTRITION: Calories 210, Fat 4, Fiber 4, Carbs 10, Protein 4

Cinnamon Apples

Preparation time: 10 minutes • Cooking time: 10 minutes • Servings: 4

INGREDIENTS

- 2teaspoons cinnamon powder
- 5apples, cored and cut into chunks
- ½ teaspoon nutmeg powder
- 1tablespoon maple syrup
- ½ cup water
- 4tablespoons vegetable oil
- ¼ cup whole wheat flour
- ¾ cup old-fashioned rolled oats
- ¼ cup coconut sugar

DIRECTIONS

1. Put the apples in a pan that fits your air fryer, add cinnamon, nutmeg, maple syrup and water.
2. Add oil mixed with oats, sugar and flour, stir, spread on top of the apples, introduce in your air fryer, cook at 350 degrees F for 10 minutes and

serve them warm.

3. Enjoy!

NUTRITION: Calories 180, Fat 6, Fiber 8, Carbs 19,
Protein 12

Carrot and Pineapple Cinnamon Bread

Preparation time: 10 minutes • Cooking time: 45 minutes • Servings: 6

INGREDIENTS

- 5ounces whole wheat flour
- ¾ teaspoon baking powder
- ½ teaspoon baking soda
- ½ teaspoon cinnamon powder
- ¼ teaspoon nutmeg, ground
- 1tablespoon flax meal combined with 2 tablespoons water
- 3tablespoons coconut cream
- ½ cup sugar
- ¼ cup pineapple juice
- 4tablespoons sunflower oil
- 1/3 cup carrots, grated
- 1/3 cup pecans, toasted and chopped
- 1/3 cup coconut flakes, shredded
- Cooking spray

DIRECTIONS:

1. In a bowl, mix flour with baking soda and powder, salt, cinnamon and nutmeg and stir.
2. In another bowl, mix flax meal with coconut cream, sugar, pineapple juice, oil, carrots, pecans

and coconut flakes and stir well.

3. Combine the two mixtures and stir well, pour into a springform pan greased with cooking spray, transfer to your air fryer and cook on 320 degrees F for 45 minutes.

4. Leave the cake to cool down, cut and serve it.

5. Enjoy!

NUTRITION: Calories 180, Fat 6, Fiber 2, Carbs 12, Protein 4

Cocoa and Coconut Bars

Preparation time: 10 minutes • Cooking time: 14 minutes • Servings: 12

INGREDIENTS

- 6ounces coconut oil, melted
- 3tablespoons flax meal combined with 3 tablespoons water
- 3ounces cocoa powder
- 2teaspoons vanilla
- ½ teaspoon baking powder
- 4ounces coconut cream
- 5tablespoons coconut sugar

DIRECTIONS

1. In a blender, mix flax meal with oil, cocoa powder, baking powder, vanilla, cream and sugar and pulse.
2. Pour this into a lined baking dish that fits your air fryer, introduce in the fryer at 320 degrees F, bake for 14 minutes, slice into rectangles and serve.
3. Enjoy!

NUTRITION: Calories 178, Fat 14, Fiber 2, Carbs 12, Protein 5

Vanilla Cake

Preparation time: 10 minutes • Cooking time: 25 minutes • Servings: 12

INGREDIENTS

- 6tablespoons black tea powder
- 2cups almond milk, heated
- 2cups coconut sugar
- 3tablespoons flax meal combined with 3 tablespoons water
- 2teaspoons vanilla extract
- ½ cup vegetable oil
- 3and ½ cups whole wheat flour
- 1teaspoon baking soda
- 3teaspoons baking powder

DIRECTIONS

1. In a bowl, mix heated milk with tea powder, stir and leave aside for now.
2. In a larger bowl, mix the oil with sugar, flax meal, vanilla extract, baking powder, baking soda and flour and stir everything really well.
3. Add tea and milk mix, stir well and pour into a greased cake pan.
4. Introduce in the fryer, cook at 330 degrees F for 25 minutes, leave aside to cool down, slice and serve it.

5. Enjoy!

NUTRITION: Calories 180, Fat 4, Fiber 4, Carbs 6, Protein 2

Sweet Apple Cupcakes

Preparation time: 10 minutes • Cooking time: 20 minutes • Servings: 4

INGREDIENTS

- 4tablespoons vegetable oil
- 3tablespoons flax meal combined with 3 tablespoons water
- ½ cup pure applesauce
- 2teaspoons cinnamon powder
- 1teaspoon vanilla extract
- 1apple, cored and chopped
- 4teaspoons maple syrup
- ¾ cup whole wheat flour
- ½ teaspoon baking powder

DIRECTIONS

1. Heat up a pan with the oil over medium heat, add applesauce, vanilla, flax meal and maple syrup, stir, take off heat and cool down.
2. Add flour, cinnamon, baking powder and apples, whisk, pour into a cupcake pan, introduce in your air fryer at 350 degrees F and bake for 20 minutes.
3. Transfer cupcakes to a platter and serve them warm.
4. Enjoy!

NUTRITION: Calories 200, Fat 3, Fiber 1, Carbs 5, Protein 4

Conclusion

Thank you for making it through to the end of ***Super Easy Air Fryer Cookbook: A Complete Cookbook To Prepare Better, Tastier And Faster Air Fryer Dishes For Yourself And Your Family*** , let's hope it was informative and able to provide you with all of the tools you need to achieve your goals whatever they may be.

The **Air Fryer** may take some time to get accustomed to. It takes time to determine new habits and become familiar with food replacement methods, including how to make low-cost food tasty and satisfying.

But if you keep up with it, it can become a replacement way of life that is natural and budget-friendly. It can also lead to some important health improvements, especially if you are suffering from any condition, keto diet proves to be helpful. And better health can mean fewer doctor visits and lower medical costs.

Finally, if you found this book useful in any way, a review is always appreciated!

CPSIA information can be obtained
at www.ICGtesting.com
Printed in the USA
BVHW041444020321
601493BV00011B/790

9 781801 947398